Integrating Change and Embracing It!

Utilizing Strategic Planning

By

Richard D. Montanye

ISBN: 1-4107-6261-0 (e-book)
ISBN: 1-4107-6262-9 (Paperback)

Library of Congress Control Number: 2003093866

This book is printed on acid free paper.

Printed in the United States of America
Bloomington, IN

1stBooks - rev. 08/06/03

Dedication

This book is dedicated to those individuals that assisted me when I failed, guided me in the right direction and mentored me when I needed it most.

I would like to thank my beautiful wife for her loving support and encouragement in writing this book and supporting my career.

Foreward

I wrote this book as a result of all the seminars, meetings, charity events and business functions that I have attended.

Everyone talks about vision, goals, teamwork, change, mission and strategic planning. No one really talks in detail, how to consolidate all of this into a successful strategic plan and integrate it into an organization.

I provide a different way of thinking and getting change implemented with staff supporting the change. I do have considerable knowledge in combining all of these elements into a well written strategic plan that gets results and acceptance throughout the majority of the organization.

I've used this technique in two countries and five different industries: oil and gas; government; courier service; health care and the hospitality business. No one in corporate America will have a one hundred percent acceptance. Executive teams just want to achieve getting the majority to accept.

With this book, my goal is to provide some guidance to corporations, departments, executives, managers and employees on how to write and go about creating a successful strategic plan that will get results and get change underway with the majority of the company accepting it.

Introduction

"Give us the tools, and we will finish the job." - Winston Churchill

Integrating change and embracing it is done through communication, involving as many employees as possible and selling it to your stakeholders. To integrate change into a corporation seamlessly, it should be done utilizing strategic planning. Done correctly, this process can make the toughest goals seem effortless. This requires everyone to have an open mind, think outside of the box, and allows the departments to have the freedom to come up with goals to achieve the mission and a vision statement reflecting the strategic plan. This will leave the departments with the tough question. How do we get there? What you read is correct; let the departments come up with the goals. This is mentioned later in the book. Strategic plan goals are the change agents that will be implemented to move a company forward.

You will see the word stakeholder throughout this book and here is the definition for it:

Stakeholder—anyone who has a vested interest in a company's success. This could be your employees, customers, partners, vendors, creditors and shareholders.

I continue to fine tune and improve this process as I continue my knowledge of learning about different industries and learning more about the most valued corporate assets, its stakeholders. I enjoy working with people, sharing my vision with them and watching them jump on the bandwagon to improve performance. In this book, I plan to lay out the groundwork to show anyone from entry level to executive level positions how to integrate change and get people you work with to embrace it. Done properly, this will work for both small and large corporations.

Table of Contents

Chapter One
Strategic Plan
(The Corporate Bible)

"An empowered organization is one in which individuals have the knowledge, skill, desire, and opportunity to personally succeed in a way that leads to collective organizational success." - Stephen R. Covey, Principle-centered Leadership

In this chapter, we will dissect the Strategic Plan and show how it is used to incorporate change. This is the hardest of all plans. Some people have a knack for this and some have to work at it. I had a professor tell me one day that in order to succeed in the corporate world, take as many English and writing courses as possible. This has been preached to many generations; only a few listen and actually do it! Once I heard those words, I could envision where I wanted to be in the corporate world.

Strategic planning is a process that requires vision and the ability to assess where you are today and know where you want to be three to five years down the line. This capability does not come easily. It's the same thing as viewing a run down house. Some will envision the potential and some will just see a run down house and not be able to get beyond that vision.

This is a gift many leaders have. The ability to go into a place and evaluate where the company, department, section and employees are today, compared to its peers. They know where they want to

1

go and can see it come together with each departments help. How do leaders do this? Leaders meet with departments and employees in their area and listen to what they have to say and ask questions. This is how the vision statement is created.

The goal is to convey the message to the company and have the company see the same vision and have the same enthusiasm to reach the milestones. By having a strategic plan, change takes place, moves the company forward and meets its financial goals by participation from stakeholders and shared communication about the plan.

Failure occurs when there are no visions, goals or communication in place to get the point across of what the company is trying to achieve.

The Strategic Plan should be specific as to the goals it wants to reach. I've seen vague goals in corporations that say, "They want to be in the top percentile of their group.". What does that mean to a department in the organization. How does that affect what they are doing in the computer room, finance, marketing, rates, mailroom and etc…

A strategic plan can and should be implemented at every level of the corporation. This process takes about three to six months to develop when every level is involved. It's a good habit to incorporate this from the executive level to the entry level. Each plan should build upon each other. This does three things.

- You are teaching a valuable lesson to your employees by encouraging them to see the vision and have visions of their own

- Employees take ownership of their respective areas
- Morale will improve

To build a workable strategic plan and integrate change, every individual in the company, departments and sections must be given the opportunity to participate.

Certain levels will have the final say as to what can be accomplished through the proper process and what goals are going to be achieved. Not everyone can have input in everything that encompasses the Strategic Plan.

Company Level/Executive Level

The Executive level is where the course of success is determined. At this level, blueprints are made for the strategic plan. The blueprints are a rough estimate of the goals that need to be accomplished. Before it is handed down to lower management to create goals in alignment with achieving the mission and vision statements, the executive team needs to determine the following:

- Dates Covered (Three to Five Years)
- Mission Statement
- Vision Statement

The executive team consists of the following: Chief Executive Officer, President, Chief Financial Officer, Chief Information Officer, Vice Presidents and

Directors.   This is the prime time for support
departments to show they can contribute to a
company's success.

Department Level

The department directors are a part of the executive
team who work on the mission and vision statements.
The department director conveys the mission and
vision statements to the department and collects the
goals from the department manager and places them in
the strategic plan for review. The director is the link
between upper and lower management.   They keep
upper management updated on the progress being
made in the departments and inform the departments
what the expectations are of upper management.

Managers need the freedom to resolve issues
anyway they can within their means to reach the goals
of the strategic plan.

Section Level

The section manager or team leader works at the
department level to find out what the mission and
vision statements are that need to be reached.   This
level determines what goals will be required to achieve
the statements.   Who better should come up with the
goals than the ones who have to achieve and
implement them.

The manager will decide on what resources are
needed, such as training, costs and time line to

accomplish the goals. He or she does not dictate when the goals will be accomplished, just how long it will take to accomplish the goals.

When creating goals, be generic as to what will be done, not the tools required to accomplish the goal (See example). If this level does not exist, then it is the department level's responsibility to provide this information.

Example: **Goal:** XYZ - Will investigate and select a reporting tool that will automate the reporting process and send it via the web or e-mail to the appropriate person for review.

In the example above, it was not specific as to what program or tools will be utilized, just what will be accomplished by automating this process. It does not mention how the goals will be achieved. A company does not care how the goals are achieved as long as they fall within three guidelines: the process is within budget, time frame and it is legal. The reason a program or tool was not selected is because these things change constantly.

Individual Level

The employees work with both the section manager and department manager to determine how they can contribute to reaching the mission and vision statements of the company. Employees will also inform the team leader or managers of any additional training they will require to accomplish the goals, they will also provide an estimate of how long it will take to complete the goals.

Employees need the tools to do their job. If they are not given the tools, how can they be held accountable?

Chapter Two
Make-up of the Strategic Plan

"...As we, the leaders, deal with tomorrow, our task is not to try to make perfect plans.

...Our task is to create organizations that are sufficiently flexible and versatile that they can take our imperfect plans and make them work in execution. That is the essential character of the learning organization." - Gordon R. Sullivan & Michael V. Harper

The strategic plan is a collection of ideas and processes that every level should have input, to achieve the mission and vision statements. The Strategic Plan should incorporate the following:

- Dates Covered (Three to Five Years)
- Mission Statement
- Vision Statement
- Goals
- Summary

Dates Covered (Three to Five Years)

I've seen several strategic plans that covered three years and five years. I myself prefer three years, anything longer than that is hard to predict. There are many variables that come into play that can change the course of your plan. It does not matter if it is three or five years. Outside variables can cause problems and will require the company to be flexible in a changing environment. This is mentioned later in the book.

Ensure you have the time span to coincide with your budget cycle, (calendar or fiscal year). This will help ensure the dollars are there to fund each goal and will make the budget process much easier.

Mission Statement

Every strategic plan needs to have a mission statement of what the company is all about, what is it trying to achieve, and the values it places inside and outside the company.

It is a good idea for each department to have a mission statement of its own to ensure it is in alignment with the company's mission and vision statements and that the department is collaborating with other departments to achieve its goals.

Vision Statement

As mentioned above with the mission statement, a vision statement is just as important. It provides an insight of what the company is trying to achieve in the future and how it wants to be viewed by its stakeholders. It should be specific in what it wants to achieve but leave the ideas to the departments as to how those visions will come about.

It is the vision statements that will change with every new strategic plan to stay ahead of changing times. This should also occur at each department to ensure the department is getting the challenges it wants to exist. This helps morale and employee satisfaction.

Goals

It is goals that make up the strategic plan and gets change underway. Think of this as a psychological way of implementing change. By calling these goals, everyone thinks differently. They want to know how to achieve or how are we going to achieve the goals. By achieving the goals they are unknowingly making change occur throughout the company. As far as the employees are concerned, they are not changing things; they are achieving goals, which show self-fulfillment, not self-doubt about change.

Many people do not like change because change to them represents the unknown. By using the word change the following questions arise: Why are we doing this? How does this impact me?

The answer to the two-part question above is with the strategic plan. Why are we doing this? The strategic plan puts the change agent in place by having the employee aware of the mission and vision statements of what the company is trying to achieve in the next three to five years.

The other part, how does this impact me? It gets employee involved in ways they can contribute by either getting training or utilizing the experience they already have.

By answering those two questions you already have a buy-in by the employees; because the employees along with the department managers will create the goals. Every strategic plan should consist of the following for each goal:

- Goals—Does this assists the company in achieving the mission and vision statements? What needs to be done?
- Present—Where are we currently? How is it done now?
- Benefits—What will the company achieve by reaching each goal? Save time, dollars, space, better customer service and etc…
- Cost—How much will it cost to achieve these goals? This should include labor for outsourcing, advertising, hardware, software, consultants, training and etc…

These should be itemized for each goal to reflect where the dollars will be spent. Just an estimated cost is needed for these programs or tools. Increase the cost by twenty percent for a cushion. See example 1:

Example 1:
Goal: XYZ will investigate and select a document-imaging program that will assist XYZ and affiliated sites to better manage documentation.
Current: There is no document-imaging application in place. Individuals have to search within each department to find the document needed.
Benefits: Providing a document imaging application saves money on space being utilized by hard copies. Saves time and money

on retrieving files during research and audits. This allows the flexibility for everyone to retrieve electronic images (patient, employee, contracts and etc...) at their desktops.

Cost: $245,000 (Application $115,000, Servers $60,000, Consultant $60,000 Training for two $10,000)

Summary

Provide a summary of how this will be accomplished, what it will take and what will be achieved by performing the strategic plan.

Chapter Three
Communication

"Never tell people how to do things. Tell them what to do and they will surprise you with their ingenuity." - George Patton

Communication is the success or failure of any project or plan. Keeping the stakeholders involved requires many forms of communication and guarantees the success or execution of your strategic plan. Communication is priceless, easy to achieve and easily forgotten. Every plan should have communication as their number one goal, which will occur the entire length of the strategic plan. When stakeholders are not involved, it leads them to think the company/department has something to hide. This degrades company morale and causes many other issues to arise. So, stay in touch! Keeping in touch can involve but are not limited to the following:

- Board Meetings
- Department Meetings
- Staff Meetings
- Videoconferencing
- E-mail
- Letters/memos
- Company newsletters
- Personal Meetings

Board Meetings

Board meetings are a good way for the board members and the executive team to stay updated on the direction of the company and formulate the vision statement for the next strategic plan.

Department Meetings

This needs to be held by the director of the department to give insight to the managers and staff of what is happening in the company and what the plans are for the future of the company. The director would most likely have the answers to questions that may arise.

Some directors have meetings with the managers only and the managers have meetings with their staff. Already, there are too many layers before the information gets passed to the employees. The information can get turned around and everyone conveys messages differently. Some do not give enough detail or do not have the answers to questions that may arise.

Staff Meetings

Staff meetings are a great place to talk about the strategic plan and brainstorm some ideas on how to achieve them. By having the brainstorming session with the employees they know they have a part in achieving the goals and feel more connected of how this impacts them.

Videoconferencing

If you have field operations, this is a great tool to get the info out quickly to them before there are any rumors floating around. If possible, try to have the meeting with the field operation staff the same day the departmental meeting is scheduled.

E-mail

This is a great tool to disseminate information to a large amount of employees and it ensures those that did not attend the meeting to read about it later. This is the best tool for the executive team to keep employees updated on the progress being made or any obstacles that may be in the way.

Letters/Memos

Use this to keep your customers, shareholders and vendors updated on the direction of the company and the progress it is making on the strategic plan.

Company Newsletters

Not all companies have a newsletter but this would be a good place to provide information and post questions/answer sessions that other employees may have.

Personal Meetings

Personal meetings are essential to have with your employees. This is the prime opportunity to answer any questions or any insecurity they may have. This is also your time to get feedback on ways they may have to achieve those goals.

Also, have meetings with your vendors, they can provide or suggest much needed help to achieve those goals. They may also provide you contacts that you can call upon. They may have already went through the same goals you are trying to achieve. You may not like to listen to them, but they can be resourceful.

Chapter Four
Stakeholders

"A leader is someone who steps back from the entire system and tries to build a more collaborative, more innovative system that will work over the long term." - Robert Reich, Former United States Secretary of Labor

Stakeholders are companies or individuals that have a vested interest in seeing the company succeed. They are the following:

- Employees
- Shareholders
- Business Partners
- Customers
- Creditors
- Vendors

Employees

Employees have the largest vested interest in a company. I agree more and more employees are moving around every three to five years but even they need to stay in one place for a while to support their standard of living. What are employees' needs or what are they looking for? Not in any order, they are looking for a salary, medical plan, retirement, flexible schedule, challenges, stable environment and so forth.

Shareholders

Your shareholders can be anyone who has a vested interest in the company. These individuals or companies depend on your company's stock to provide for many things: retirement, college money, homes, leisure items and etc…As you can see they want your company to succeed!

Business Partners

Business partners can be silent or active. They may have personal cash involved or not. But one thing is for certain. They want to see their wealth improve as payment for the labor they put into the company or the financial backing they provide.

Customers

The customers depend on the company's success due to the contracts they have with the company or vice versa. No one wants lag time in his or her business process. Having lag time costs them dollars and they have to scramble around looking for other companies to fill the gap. Your customers may be other companies. They may be individuals the company depends on for day-to-day business or to provide cash flow.

Creditors

Creditors want money from you. This provides little explanation. The last thing they want is a company to file bankruptcy.

Vendors

Vendors want to ensure they can provide a service to you. As mentioned previously, listen to what they have to say. They may be able to help in ways you never thought possible. You may also find you can do what they are providing with your staff, in house.

Chapter Five
Taking a Risk

"The quality of a leader is reflected in the standards they set for themselves." - Ray Kroc, Fast-food franchising pioneer

Taking a risk is something we all do in our everyday life but I prefer to take calculated risks. First, I am an optimistic person. I believe in the five P's of business: Proper Planning Prevents Poor Performance. By following this slogan, I can increase my chances for success after I do the T-chart process. Here are the steps I go through:

- Risk
- T-Chart
- Positives outweigh Negatives

Risk

What is your definition of "RISK"? Is it failure? A chance to fail, most will say it is failure. As I had mentioned earlier, I'm optimistic.

The proper definition of RISK should be: An opportunity to succeed.

If you follow my definition of risk, you will dive more in depth of how to succeed than fail. Who would you want on your strategic planning team?

The first thing to take is risk. What will it take for this company, department or section to achieve our goals to reach our vision statement! Once you brainstorm and come up with several risky ideas that are legal of course, then you are ready for the next step.

T-Chart

In my opinion, T-charts are the best way to rank risky ideas. Create two columns; at the top put "pros" and "cons" or "positives" and "negatives" for each column. Write down all of the positive points about an idea and write down all the negative ones. This is just the first pass through!

Look at each negative and break them down as to why you think they are negatives. Not enough cash, manpower, resources, knowledge or management not willing to take the risk?

Breaking down each negative and finding out the root cause of why they cannot be done will give the group a more definitive answer in making a sound judgment about each idea. If the negative can be resolved then move it to the positive column.

T-charts can be used with anything when a decision has to be made. The problem is, companies and individuals fail to use them. Should I ask for this raise; should we pursue that project, should we buy this software, etc…

Positives outweigh Negatives

After completing the T-charts for all the risky ideas and breaking down each negative to find out if it's truly negative, look at the ideas in T-chart format. Do the positive outweigh the negatives? If so, the risk is in your favor to succeed and reach your goals. If not, look at one of your other ideas and break them down. Continue the process until the group is comfortable with the idea.

Chapter Six
Acceptance

"Leadership is the art of getting someone else to do something you want done because he wants to do it." - Dwight D. Eisenhower, 34th President of the United States

To get the acceptance of the employees, you are making them aware of the strategic plan and the goals it will take to achieve it. Having them involved in the process makes it that much easier for them to accept. Now that the timeline, mission, vision and goals (goal, present, benefits and costs) are defined, the executive team needs to get together to do the following:

- Meetings
- Ratings
- Calculating
- Presentation
- Approval/Buy-In

Meetings

The executive team will have many meetings throughout this process to look over the goals and to ensure they are specific in meeting the mission and vision statements. At one of the meetings, the goals need to be scrutinized in the review process. Once approved, everyone in the process has the understanding these are the goals that will move the company forward.

The executives will see where they are at present/today (this is usually an eye opener), the benefits of achieving the goals and how much is it going to cost. Once all of this is looked over and the executive team accepts the goals, then the next process is to rate them.

Ratings

The rating process is a very simple method depending on the timeline of the strategic plan, three or five years. Beside each goal rate them with a 1-5. This scale represents which year the individuals want to see that goal happen (1-1st yr, 2-2nd yr, 3-3rd yr and so on). After the goals are rated, it is time to calculate them.

Calculating

After the strategic plan is rated and collected from each member of the executive team, a calculating method must occur. I will use Microsoft Excel since that is the most widely used. This can also be done in Lotus 1-2-3.

In an excel spreadsheet in the far left column type in the year (1-3 or 1-5) in the top row type in the goals. See example 2:

Year	Goal 1	Goal 2	Goal 3	Goal 4
1				
2				
3				

Example 2

Beside each goal there is the number of a year between 1-5. Put a number 1 next to the corresponding year. See example 3

Joe's rating: Goal 1 = 2, Goal 2 = 1, Goal 3 = 2, Goal 4 = 3

Year	Goal 1	Goal 2	Goal 3	Goal 4
1		1		
2	1		1	
3				1

Example 3

With each person's response, the corresponding number will be incremented by 1. See example 4

Joe's rating: Goal 1 = 2, Goal 2 = 1, Goal 3 = 2, Goal 4 = 3
Bob's rating: Goal 1 = 3, Goal 2 = 1, Goal 3 = 2, Goal 4 = 3

Year	Goal 1	Goal 2	Goal 3	Goal 4
1		2		
2	1		2	
3	1			2

Example 4

Each goal should have the same total of responses. (Goal 1 has 2, Goal 2 has 2 and so forth.)

Once the goals have been calculated, it's time to do the graph. Highlight the years and goals and select the graph symbol and the program will walk you through the process. See example 5

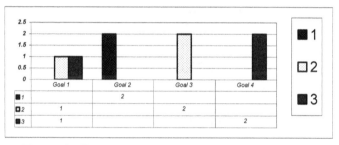

Example 5

The column on the far left represents the number of respondents. The coded bars represent the year the goal will be conducted. The legend for the coded bars is on the far right side.

Once your graph has been completed, it will be time for the presentation.

Presentation

This is the time when the executive team is presented with the results of the graphs for review.

In cases there is a tie for a goal to be completed between two different years, it is up to the executive team to decide which year the goal should be done.

Once the review process has been completed and all discrepancies worked out, it is time to organize the strategic plan. See example 6, this represents the results from example 5.

Example 6

Yr 2004-2005
Goal 2

Yr 2005-2006
Goal 3

Yr 2006-2007
Goal 1
Goal 4

Budgeting

Once the goals are organized in the years they will be completed, a budget process should start. This gives the executive team an idea of what it will cost to implement these goals within the designated time frame. The executive team needs to provide the funds necessary for the changes to take affect and propel the company and departments forward.

The cost only reflects what it costs to implement each particular goal in the strategic plan. It is not the operating or capital budget of a company or department. In the budget spreadsheet, a designated code should be used to reflect goals in a department's budget. This makes it easy to spot-check the strategic plan agendas.

Approval/Buy-In

Now that the strategic plan is completed and the team has reviewed the goals, presented the status, benefits and the cost to implement the plan, it is time to vote on the approval of the completed plan and share it with your stakeholders. Buy-in with the employees is a given because they are the ones that came up with the goals to achieve the strategic plan. They just need to know which year to implement the goals.

Chapter Seven
Implementation

"No man will make a great leader who wants to do it all himself, or to get all the credit for doing it." - Andrew Carnegie, American industrialist, philanthropist

Coming up with the goals to achieve the mission and vision statements was a difficult and long process. The executive team and the rest of the organization should feel confident they could implement the goals successfully, since the employees came up with them. The process will be trying at times, but successful. Since the goals did not come from top to bottom, but rather, the bottom up, the goals are realistic and this will eliminate any doubt as to whether the employees can achieve these goals.

The executive and management teams need to rally behind their employees to show their support and provide what ever is necessary to achieve the goals. This process was originally agreed upon when the goals were formulated. Everyone needs to stand by his or her word and give what is needed to get the job done.

Workflow Policies

Workflow policies need to be created to complement any project plan being used by various departments. Policies for resolving issues, acceptance, closure, communication, security, data integrity, work request from other areas and etc...

This will pay for itself and save considerable time when tension arise within the group. This will help keep the process flowing smoothly. Make sure everyone is aware of the location of the policies and becomes familiar with them.

Time Lines

The time line is your project plan, I use one called SPEC (Scope, Plan, Execute and Conclude). Every company has one, if not, they need to adopt one. This provides the ground work for reaching your goals and lays out every detail from each event that is required, manpower that is needed, number of delays allowed before it impacts the next event, total cost of the project, total number of days to complete the goal/project and much more.

Parts of the plan were done in creating the goals. Make sure communication with the rest of the company is there when going through the project plan process. The earlier you involve other areas the better the outcome. So include them in the scope phase of the project. Project planning is a book all its own.

Updates

Always update everyone in the process by utilizing one or several of the communication methods mentioned earlier in this book. Make sure the company is informed after each milestone and be sure to include the stakeholders in any delay or roadblocks that may occur throughout the process. I guarantee many people will be glad to assist you in resolving the issues. Remember many minds are better than one!

Outside Variables

There are many outside variables that can change your strategic plan that may affect your company climate. This could be a natural disaster, financial ramifications from a competing company, larger customer base due to unforeseen sales or service of a hot item, unexpected large growth of the company or segment, war, etc...

Changes

Changes will occur throughout the process. If they do, do not make the decisions alone! The executive team should make any changes that occur in the strategic plan. They need to ensure the funding is there or set it aside. If a new goal is to be made, allow the departments to come up with the goal. Remember, they have to embrace, complete and implement the change.

Chapter Eight
Rewards

"A leader is best when people barely know he exists, not so good when people obey and acclaim him, worse when they despise him. But of a good leader who take little when his work is done, his aim fulfilled, they will say: We did it ourselves." - Lao-Tzu, Chinese philosopher, Founder of Taoism

Rewarding is an important factor in any company or department. The problem is, it is not done enough! Rewarding the company, departments and individuals keeps morale up and provides a self worth to the department and individual. Always reward frequently and in public utilizing one of the communication tools mentioned above. Rewarding should happen after goals have been reached and to those that make it happen.

Company Goals

Company goals are milestones that are attained through collaboration by various departments, teamwork and individual sacrifices to meet deadlines. Milestones should be announced by the executive team to show their support and recognize the departments and individuals for their dedication to achieve those goals and make change occur successfully.

Employee

There are two types of employees, those that thrive for attention and those that do not care. No matter what type of employee they are, recognition should be done. It may be completing a task ahead of time, compliments from another staff or manager, saving money, personal sacrifices, etc...How the employee is rewarded is up to the manager.

Department

Departments should be recognized by the executive team to acknowledge the sacrifices or ingenuity the department came up with to reach those goals on time or ahead of time.

Company

When the company completes the goals or within six months of completing the annual goals, then some type of recognition or small party should be provided to show appreciation for the employees and for the teamwork between various departments.

Failure

Failure will occur by an individual or department throughout the process. Do not punish the individuals for failure but foster ownership of the failure by the department or individual. Failure is a miscalculation or variable that was missed in the plan. Have a meeting with the department or individual to find out what is needed to remedy the situation and get back to reaching the goals.

Conclusion

"The final test of a leader is that he leaves behind him in other men the conviction and the will to carry on...The genius of a good leader is to leave behind him a situation which common sense, without the grace of genius, can deal with successfully." - Walter Lippmann

Writing this book has given me an opportunity to reflect upon the processes that I have used to implement change and get the stakeholders to embrace it. Strategic planning was the tool that gave me the opportunity to wrap all of these things into one process. This assisted me in getting end results in the organizations and assisted me in my career growth. I will continue to use this process throughout my work life, to move our organization forward for many years to come.

What I hoped to achieve, was to show how strategic planning can be effective by wrapping all the right elements together and implementing it in an organization. Organizations, departments and employees can use strategic planning to get results, structure and focus to its mission and vision statements.

By changing the word around from change to goals, I was able to get more support from various departments and employees. Which one would you follow? Someone who said, "They have many changes that needed to be achieved for growth to occur." Or, someone who said, "They have many goals that need to be achieved for growth." They both achieve the same thing, results. People with goals seem to be the more visionary then those that require change. Employees like leaders that have vision and goals to move forward.

With that in mind, think about the words you use in your daily life to propel your ideas and career to new heights. I have worked in another country where custom barriers needed to be overcome and accepted. By becoming familiar with the other countries' business and culture customs, it was much easier to get support from different nationalities. They like to see foreigners go out of their way to learn their culture. Remember; when in Rome do as the Romans do.

Sample Layout:

Three Year Strategic Plan for XYZ

October 1, 2003 - September 30, 2006

Mission

Vision

Goals

Achieving this mission and vision requires strong goals and dedication to teamwork within XYZ and collaborating with our customers. Below are the goals to make this plan a success:

All three years and beyond:

> **Goals:**
> **Current:**
> **Benefits:**
> **Cost:**

> **Goal:**
> **Current:**
> **Benefits:**
> **Cost:**

Year One (October 2003 - September 2004)

Goal:
Current:
Benefits:
Cost:

Goal:
Current:
Benefits:
Cost:

Year Two (October 2004 - September 2005)

Goal:
Current:
Benefits:
Cost:

Goal:
Current:
Benefits:
Cost:

Year Three (October 2005 - September 2006)

Goal:
Current:
Benefits:
Cost:

Goal:
Current:
Benefits:

Summary

Biography

Richard Montanye grew up in a military family moving every three years or less to various states and to different countries. Each time his family moved, there were drastic changes they had to deal with quickly; new schools, new friends, new laws, and new cultures. This required him to adapt quickly, be independent, be more observant, ask questions and be personable.

When Richard joined the military his childhood assisted him in all the changes he had experienced. Richard served four years in the military and during that time, he had moved five times to three different states and two countries. Also, during that time he had supported his way through college and completed one of his degrees within those four years.

Richard Montanye has degrees in both business administration and computer information systems. Both fields are constantly evolving to improve employee morale and production just to name two of the most important things in any corporation. Both reflect the bottom line. Richard is accustomed to change and implementing it.

Over the past fifteen years Richard has worked in two countries and five different industries (government, hospitality, gas service, courier service and healthcare) in which he overcame language and cultural barriers to implement change and challenged the way things were done. In each industry it was embraced and accepted, some with fan fare and some with out. With each move, Richard has moved up the corporate ladder doing what he enjoys best, dealing with stakeholders and turning departments and companies around. Strategic planning provided the mechanism to turn companies and departments around and provide focus to its goals.

This is a process that Richard enjoys sharing and he really wants to assist other individuals achieve their goals in their professional career. Life is about leaving the world a little better and influencing others to do better. That is what Richard wants to achieve!

The other half of this book is left blank intentionally for training purposes only, upon request.

To schedule public speaking engagements or class training, please contact First Books Library at: 1-888-519-5121.